HORSEPOWER

PICKUP
TRUCKS

by Sarah L. Schuette

Reading Consultant:

Barbara J. Fox
Reading Specialist
North Carolina State University

Capstone
press

Mankato, Minnesota

Blazers is published by Capstone Press,
151 Good Counsel Drive, P.O. Box 669, Mankato, Minnesota 56002.
www.capstonepress.com

Library of Congress Cataloging-in-Publication Data
Schuette, Sarah L., 1976–
    Pickup trucks / by Sarah L. Schuette.
    p. cm.—(Blazers. Horsepower)
    Summary: "Describes pickup trucks, their main features, and
how they are raced"—Provided by publisher.
    Includes bibliographical references and index.
    ISBN-13: 978-0-7368-5474-0 (hardcover)
    ISBN-10: 0-7368-5474-6 (hardcover)
    ISBN-13: 978-0-7368-6895-2 (softcover pbk.)
    ISBN-10: 0-7368-6895-X (softcover pbk.)
    1. Pickup trucks—Juvenile literature. 2. Truck racing—Juvenile
literature. I. Title. II. Series.
TL230.15.S4 2006
629.223'2—dc22   2005026185

Editorial Credits

Mandy Marx, editor; Jason Knudson, set designer; Thomas Emery,
    book designer; Jo Miller, photo researcher; Scott Thoms,
    photo editor

Photo Credits

Artemis Images, 15, 27
Courtesy of American Honda Motor Co. Inc., 5, 6, 7 (both), 8, 24
Getty Images Inc./Jamie Squire, 26; Scott Olson, cover
Index Stock Imagery, 10–11; Randy Lorentzen, 23
Mercury Press International/Isaac Hernandez, 12, 14, 21 (top)
Ron Kimball Stock/Ron Kimball, 13, 16–17, 18–19, 20, 21 (bottom),
    28–29

The author dedicates this book to Brown T. Schuette of
Belle Plaine, Minnesota.

1 2 3 4 5 6 11 10 09 08 07 06

TABLE OF CONTENTS

ROAD TESTS

New pickup trucks face difficult road tests before they can be sold. They are pushed to their limits of speed and handling.

During road tests, pickups pull heavy loads. They climb and splash through rugged areas.

Pickup speed is timed on a test track. Once new models pass road tests, they are ready to be sold.

POWERFUL TRUCKS

Pickups are built to be powerful and tough. Full-size pickups have heavy frames, large tires, and deep beds.

Some pickup trucks have powerful hemi engines. These engines guzzle lots of gas. They produce more than 300 horsepower.

BLAZER FACT

Horsepower measures engine power. The term "horsepower" came from comparing engine power to a horse's strength.

Wheel base

Pickups have the power to haul loads twice their size. Pickups use hitches to tow. A wide wheel base helps them support heavy loads.

BLAZER FACT

Full-size pickups weigh more than 5,500 pounds (2,495 kilograms). That's more than 10 grizzly bears.

Hitch

Bed

Tailgate

Cab

COMPACTS AND CROSSOVERS

Compact trucks have short beds and bodies. They look like mini versions of full-size pickup trucks.

Crossover vehicles are part car
and part pickup truck. They look
like SUVs or cars with cargo beds.

Nissan Frontier

Chevrolet SSR

AT WORK AND PLAY

Not much can stand in the way of pickup trucks. They plow through sand, water, and mud without getting stuck.

Pickup beds are tough enough to haul heavy loads. Tailgates can swing open for easy unloading.

Some people race pickup trucks. Drivers tear around tracks and dirt courses. Whether at work or play, pickups are powerful machines.

BLAZER FACT

Pickup truck racers compete in the NASCAR Craftsman Truck Series races.

ROUGH AND TOUGH!

GLOSSARY

bed (BED)—the flat area in the back of a pickup used to carry cargo

course (KORSS)—a route

hitch (HICH)—the connection between a vehicle and an object that is pulled

horsepower (HORSS-pou-ur)—a unit for measuring engine power

SUV (ess-yoo-VEE)—a four-wheel-drive vehicle with a roomy interior, made for off-road travel; SUV stands for sport utility vehicle.

tailgate (TALE-gate)—a gate at the back of a truck that can open to the bed

wheel base (WEEL BAYSS)—the distance between the wheels on the left and right sides of a vehicle

READ MORE

Bingham, Caroline. *Truck-Mania!* Vehicle-Mania. Milwaukee: Gareth Stevens, 2004.

Savage, Jeff. *The World's Fastest Pro Stock Trucks.* Built for Speed. Mankato, Minn.: Capstone Press, 2003.

Zuehlke, Jeffrey. *Pickup Trucks.* Pull Ahead Books. Minneapolis: Lerner, 2005.

INTERNET SITES

FactHound offers a safe, fun way to find Internet sites related to this book. All of the sites on FactHound have been researched by our staff.

Here's how:

1. Visit *www.facthound.com*
2. Type in this special code **0736854746** for age-appropriate sites. Or, enter a search word related to this book for a more general search.
3. Click on the **Fetch It** button.

FactHound will fetch the best sites for you!

INDEX